Moms Needed Bread! The Women's March on Versailles

History 4th Grade

Children's European History

Speedy Publishing LLC

40 E. Main St. #1156

Newark, DE 19711

www.speedypublishing.com

Copyright 2017

All Rights reserved. No part of this book may be reproduced or used in any way or form or by any means whether electronic or mechanical, this means that you cannot record or photocopy any material ideas or tips that are provided in this book

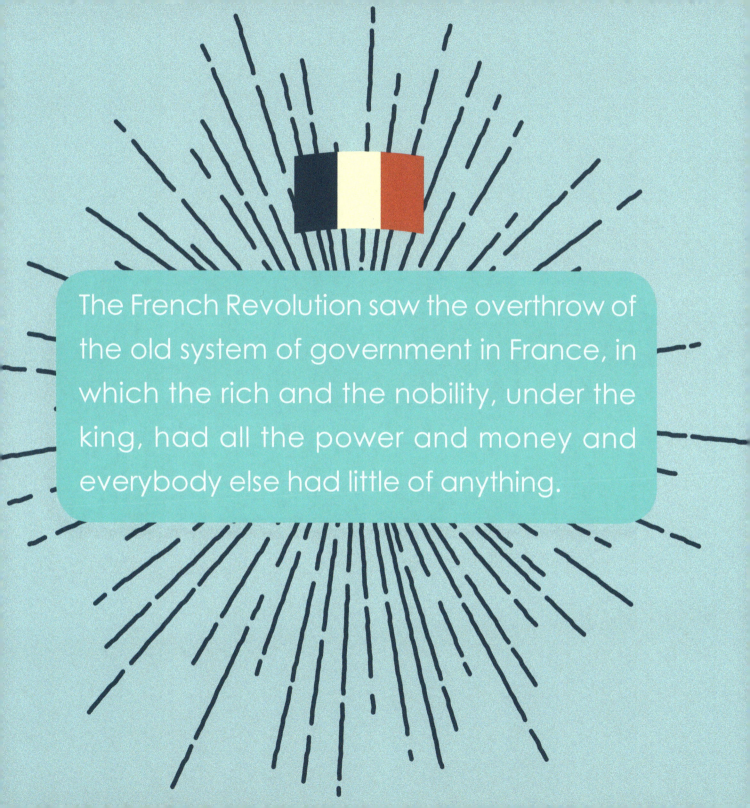

The French Revolution saw the overthrow of the old system of government in France, in which the rich and the nobility, under the king, had all the power and money and everybody else had little of anything.

At the start of the Revolution, there was a march of women that helped change everything. Learn more here about the Women's March on Versailles!

PEASANT FAMILY

THE BAKER AND HIS WIFE

In the years leading up to 1789, France had experienced droughts and poor harvests. The price of all foods went up, but the cost of bread came to stand for the cost of everything. Poor people had to spend almost half their income just for the basics like bread!

People started calling King Louis XVI "the baker", so they could criticize him without being arrested for treason. The queen, Marie-Antoinette, was called "the baker's wife".

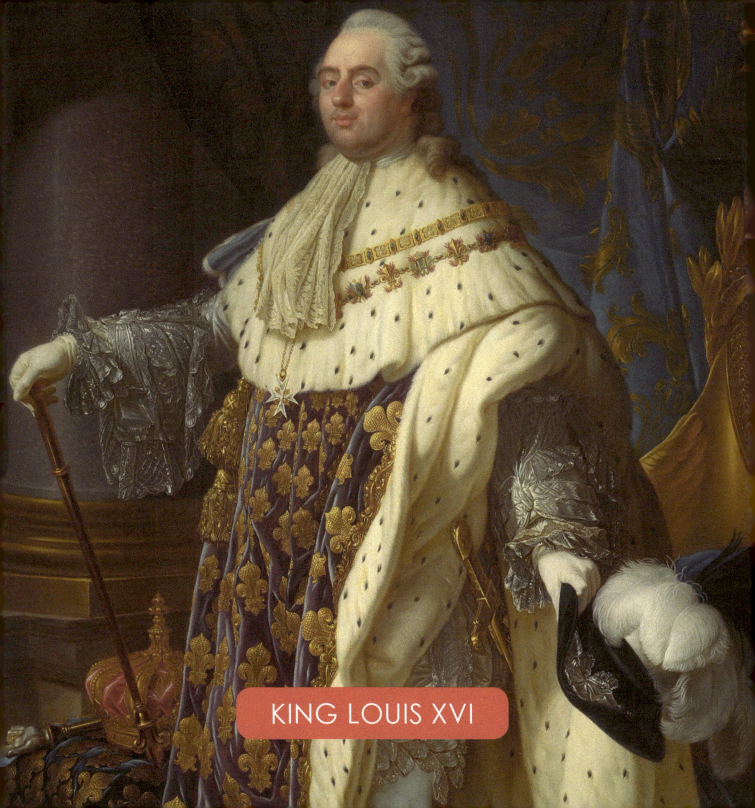

LOUIS XVI WITH THE POOR

People started to demand that the baker and his wife provide the bread they needed. They meant not just bread, but food of all sorts, clean water and, by extension, human rights like the rights to free speech and representative government.

At this time Louis was trying to establish some modest reforms to government and taxation, including getting more money from the rich nobility. But people throughout the country were upset, hungry, and afraid, and the time for modest reforms had passed.

NATIONAL ASSEMBLY TAKING THE TENNIS COURT OATH

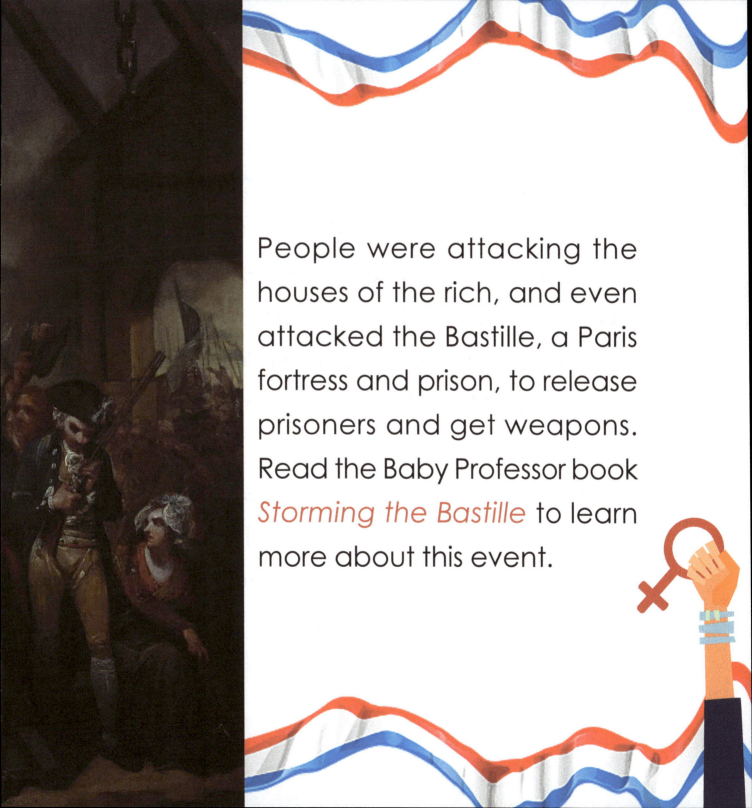

People were attacking the houses of the rich, and even attacked the Bastille, a Paris fortress and prison, to release prisoners and get weapons. Read the Baby Professor book *Storming the Bastille* to learn more about this event.

The king called a meeting of legislators at his country palace at Versailles to work on changes to the laws. In Paris, the center of the young revolution, people were afraid that the king and his friends would have too much influence, and the changes would be too small to really help anybody or to change who held power in France.

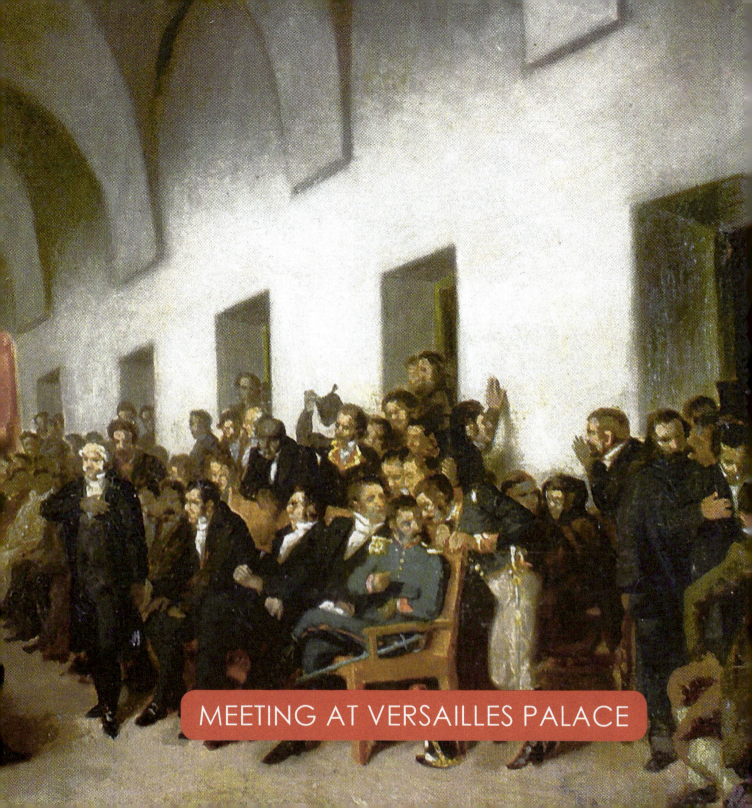
MEETING AT VERSAILLES PALACE

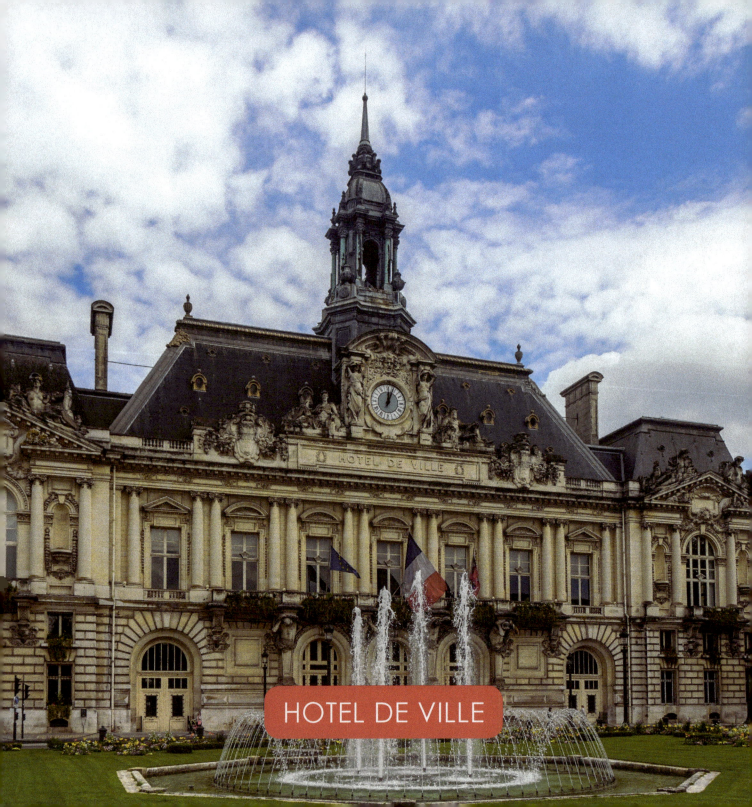

GOING TO MEET THE BAKER

Leaders of the Revolution had talked about and planned some sort of huge demonstration to get the king's attention, but it was ordinary people who actually did it. On October 5, 1789, women upset about the high price of bread starting beating drums and banging on cook pots in one of the markets in the east end of Paris.

They decided to march on the city hall, the Hôtel de Ville, to demand bread and other essentials.

The march started with a few hundred women and some men. By the time it reached the Hôtel de Ville it was a mob of over six thousand people. As the march drew toward its goal, church bells rang out an alert to bring other people.

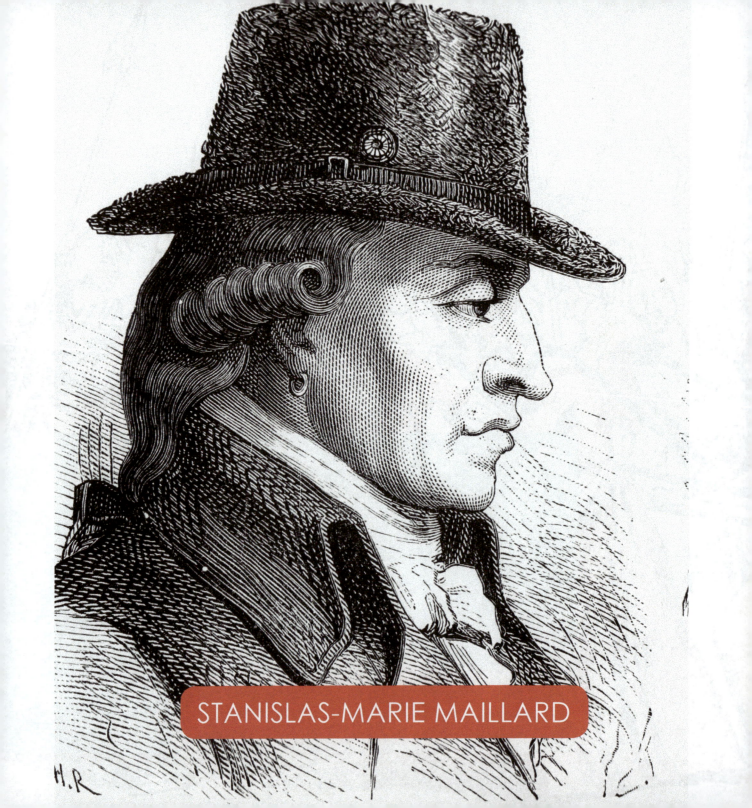
STANISLAS-MARIE MAILLARD

The marchers had few or no guns, but they had clubs, knives, and other makeshift weapons. By the time they got to city hall, they wanted not only bread, but guns.

Among the marchers was Stanislas-Marie Maillard, a popular leader. As the mob broke into the Hôtel de Ville and took hold of its food supplies and any weapons it could find, Maillard and others worked hard to convince people not to burn the building down or kill city officials.

Maillard and others started the chant, "To Versailles!" and the mob took it up. Their argument was not with the mayor or his people, but with the king. It was raining hard as the mob set out for the six-hour march to Versailles.

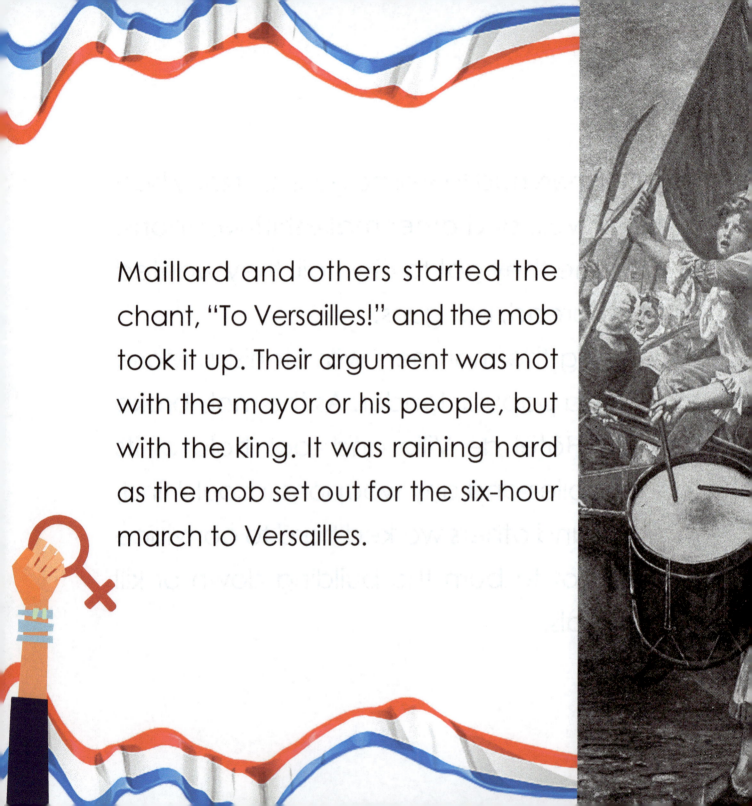

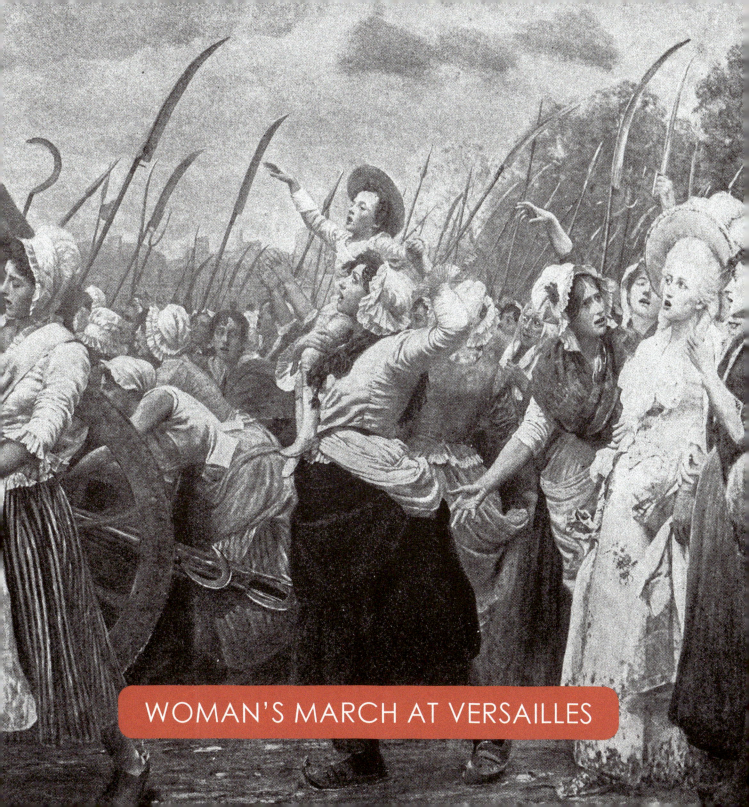
WOMAN'S MARCH AT VERSAILLES

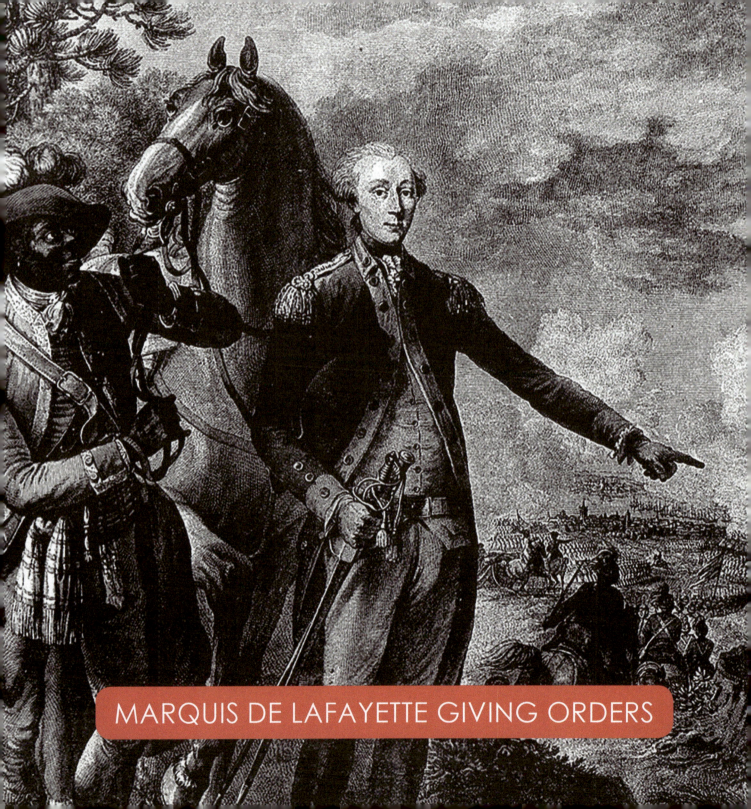

MARQUIS DE LAFAYETTE GIVING ORDERS

Soldiers of the National Guard were assembling in a Paris square to respond to the crisis. When the Marquis de Lafayette, their commander, got there, he found that many or most of the soldiers actually wanted to join the march, not stop it! (To learn more about the Marquis de Lafayette, read the Baby Professor book, *The Marquis de Lafayette: The Hero of Two Worlds*.)

Lafayette sent riders ahead to warn the king that the mob, now over ten thousand strong, was coming. The mayor's officials asked Lafayette to lead his troops with the march so he could be on hand to keep violence from breaking out. They asked if he could convince the king to return to Paris, which might give the people a sense of progress.

LOUIS XVI ENTERING PARIS

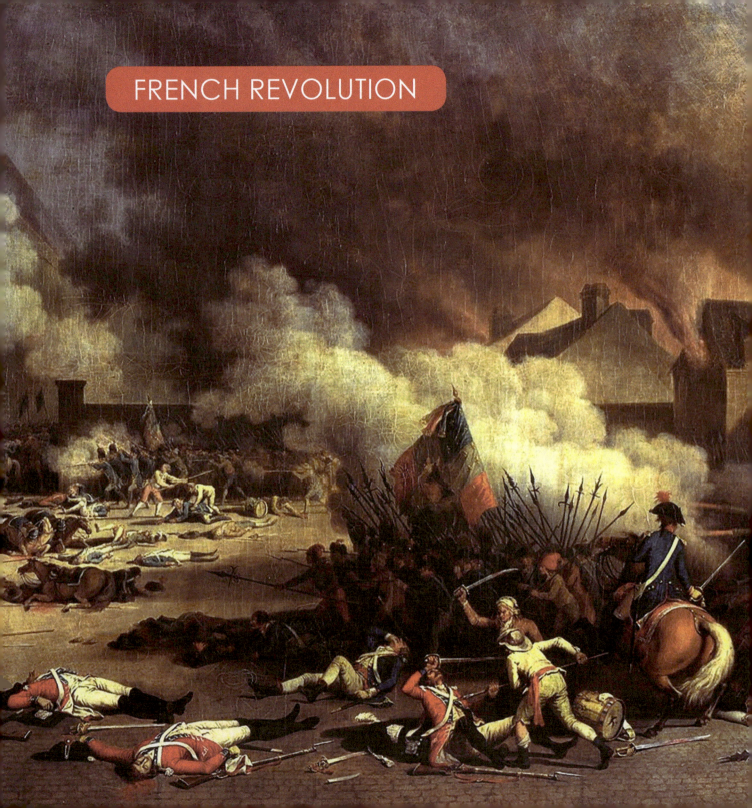
FRENCH REVOLUTION

Lafayette agreed, and led fifteen thousand troops out to Versailles, following the mob. He no longer hoped to stop the mob, but did hope the reduce the chance of violence and perhaps keep the king safe.

AT VERSAILLES

When the mob got to Versailles, they demanded to see the king so he could hear their demands. The king agreed to meet with a small group of women.

CAPTURE OF THE BASTILLE

The king listened sympathetically and promised to provide food from what was on hand at the palace, and to get more food for them in the future. Later in the day the king went out on a balcony and addressed as much of the mob as could hear them. He promised again to provide more food.

But by now people would not accept just promises. The crowd demanded that the king return to Paris, where they could keep an eye on him, and he agreed. Then the crowd demanded to see the Queen, Marie-Antoinette.

When she first became queen, Marie-Antoinette was very popular. But she came to be a symbol of all that was wrong with the nobility who ruled France.

MARIE ANTOINETTE

People blamed her, an Austrian, for many of the troubles France was suffering, and they were offended by stories of huge banquets and night-long dances, gambling parties, expensive gifts and inappropriate actions in hidden rooms in the palace. The Baby Professor book, *Marie Antoinette and her Lavish Parties*, describes the queen's lavish lifestyle.

Some people got into the palace by a rear gate, and hunted through the building looking for the queen. They broke into her private suite, and she narrowly escaped them by using a hidden door and a secret passage. Some who tried to protect the palace were killed by the mob, and some of the demonstrators also died.

Finally the queen and her children came out on a balcony. Some people in the mob pointed guns at her. But then Lafayette, who was a popular war hero, stepped on to the balcony, knelt down, and kissed the queen's hand. This helped turn the crowd away from violence.

The leaders of the Revolution, many of whom had been meeting at Versailles to plan a new constitution for France, mingled with the mob, listening to their complaints and encouraging them to not let the king try to slip out of his promises. The leaders included Robespierre, Marat, and Mirabeau—you can learn more about them in the Baby Professor book *They Got Involved! The Famous People During the French Revolution.*

MAXIMILIEN ROBESPIERRE

THE RETURN OF THE ROYAL FAMILY TO PARIS

BACK TO PARIS

The next day, October 6, the mob escorted the king, his family, and about one hundred of the deputies who had been working on the constitution out of Versailles and back to Paris. Lafayette led the procession with the National Guard.

The mob was now over sixty thousand people. Many were soldiers who had joined the march with their weapons. Some men carried long poles: on the end of the poles were the heads of some of the king's troops and servants that they had killed at Versailles. On a happier note, many of the National Guard marched with loaves of bread stuck on their bayonets!

ROYAL FAMILY IN PRISON

As the march went on, some of those with guns fired in celebration, sometimes aiming as close as they could to the carriage carrying the king. The mob called the king "Good Papa", but nobody thought that there was no danger, or that the king still held the power that he had held even a day before.

When the procession came to Paris, it delivered the king and his family to the old Tuileries Palace, on a square near the center of the city. It was a palace, but it was quite run down. On the other hand, it was right in the middle of the revolutionary population, and that's where the people wanted to keep the king so he would not run off or go back on his promises.

MARIE ANTOINETTE AND CHILDRENS AT TUILERIES PALACE

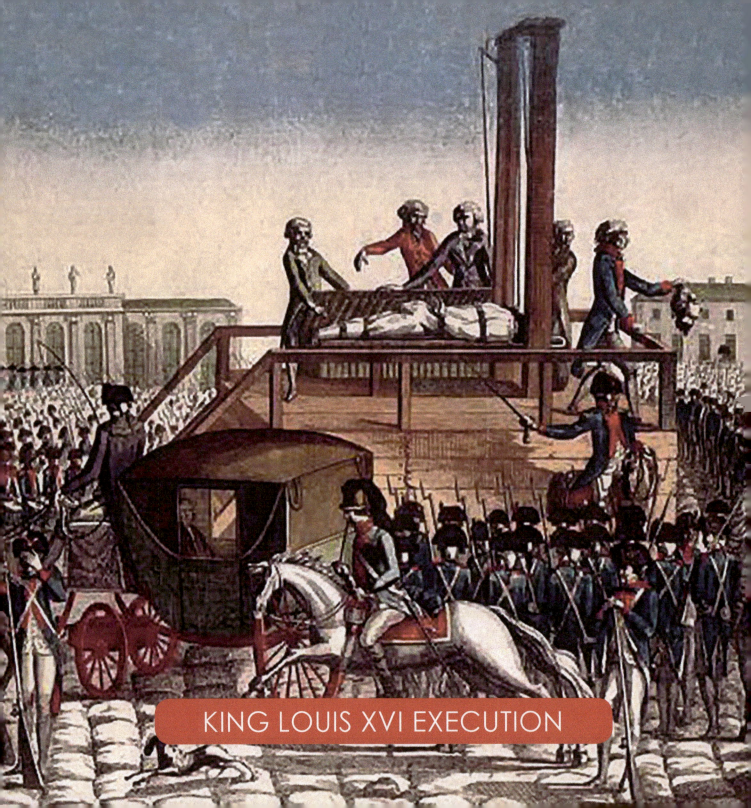
KING LOUIS XVI EXECUTION

The king understood well both the symbolism and the facts of his move back to Paris. He now made requests instead of giving orders, and he asked for a history of the life and death of England's King Charles I. Charles had been overthrown and executed about 150 years earlier, and now Louis XVI began to anticipate what might happen to him.

The king and his family stayed under close control, except for one attempt to escape, until 1793. Then Louis XVI was executed for "crimes against the nation". Marie-Antoinette was executed about nine months later.

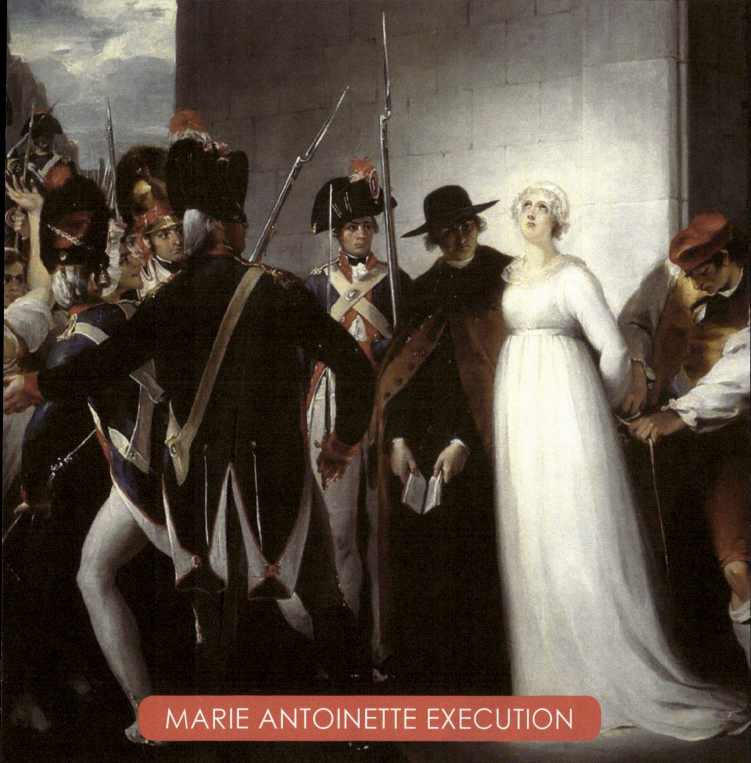
MARIE ANTOINETTE EXECUTION

For France, the Women's March was a huge symbol of the power of the common people. It inspired participants in during the French Revolution, and continues to inspire people involved in struggles for human rights today. The march, and forcing the king to come back to Paris, ended for all time the illusion that the king was all-powerful. The French royalty never recovered from this defeat.

Read other Baby Professor books, like *Are You With Us or Against Us? Looking Back on the Reign of Terror* and *The French Revolution: People Power in Action*, to learn more about these exciting times.

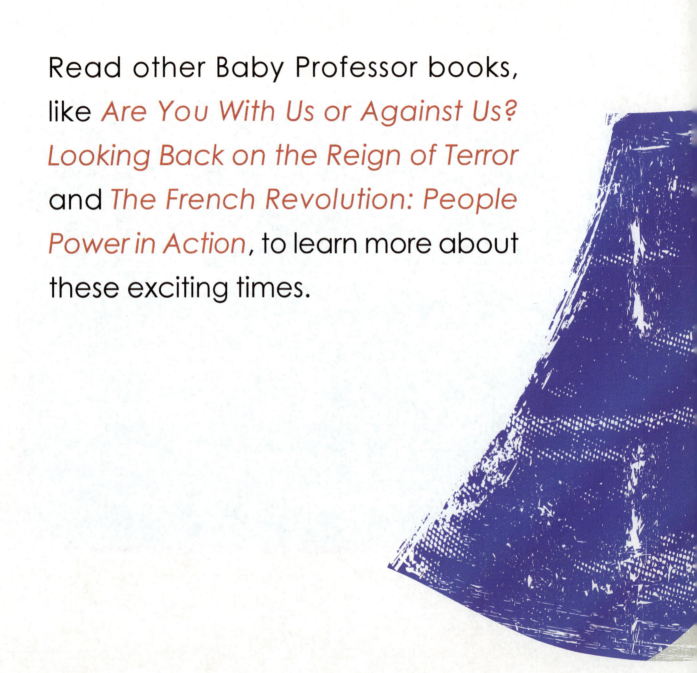

Milton Keynes UK
Ingram Content Group UK Ltd.
UKHW050924310824
447642UK00002B/97